D1613750

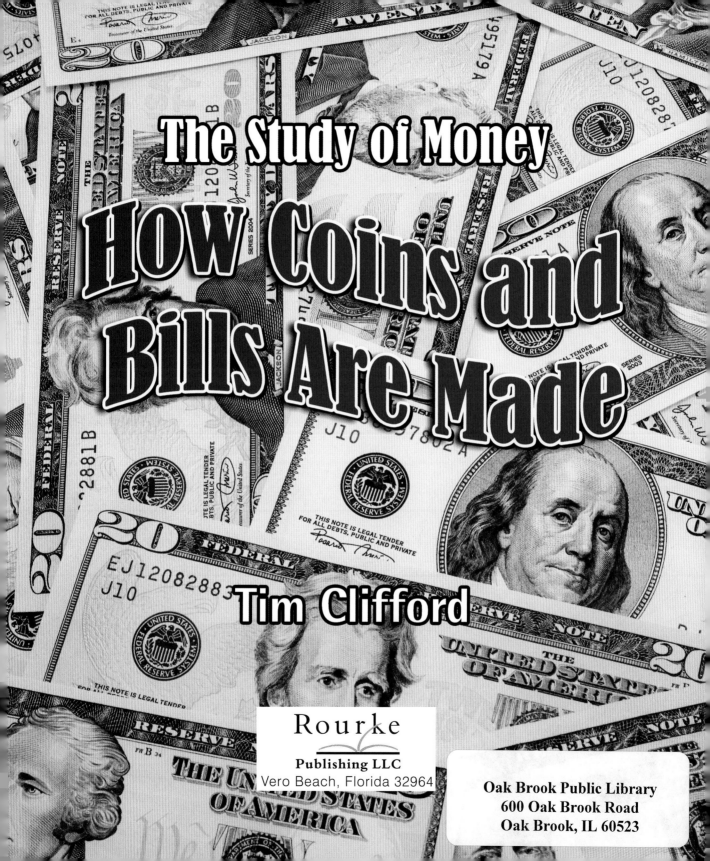

The Study of Money

How Coins and Bills Are Made

Tim Clifford

Rourke
Publishing LLC
Vero Beach, Florida 32964

Oak Brook Public Library
600 Oak Brook Road
Oak Brook, IL 60523

© 2009 Rourke Publishing LLC

All rights reserved. No part of this book may be reproduced or used in any form or by any means, electronic or mechanical, including photocopying, recording, or by any information storage and retrieval system without permission in writing from the publisher.

www.rourkepublishing.com

PHOTO CREDITS:© Library of Congress: page 4, 5 left; © Jonathan Larsen: page 5 right; © Kathy Burns/ Millyard: 6, 7 bottom; © Les Byerley: 7 top left; © Onetwo1: 7 top right; © Rich Koele: page 8; © Associated Press/ Jacqueline Larma: page 9; © U.S. Mint: page 10; © Vova Pomortzeff: page 11; © Greg Nicholas: page 13; © Michael Coddington: page 14 top; © Associated Press/ Jack Dempsey: page 14 bottom; © Associated Press/ Brad C. Bower: page 15; © George D.: page 19; © U.S. Bureau of Printing and Engraving: page 20, 24 bottom, 26; © microstocker, © Arkady Mazor, © Nikolay Okhitin, © Kanwarjit Singh Boparai, © Karen Struthers, © Valentin Mosichev, Joel Bitt: page 21; © Yakobchuk Vasyl: page 22; © Yuriy Chertok: page 23; © Christophe Testi: page 24 top; © Associated Press/ Doug Mills: page 25; © Associated Press/ Hillery Smith Garrison: page 27; © Armentrout: page 29

Editor: Jeanne Sturm

Cover Design: Renee Brady

Page Design: Tara Raymo

Library of Congress Cataloging-in-Publication Data

Clifford, Tim, 1959-
  How coins and bills are made / Tim Clifford.
      p. cm. -- (The study of money)
   ISBN 978-1-60472-404-2
  1. Money--United States--Juvenile literature. 2. Coins--United
States--Juvenile literature. 3. Paper money--United States--Juvenile
literature. I. Title.
   HG501.C643 2009
   737.40973--dc22
                                            2008011331

Printed in the USA

IG/IG

Table of Contents

History of United States Coins and Bills

A thirty dollar continental currency printed in 1778.

We are all familiar with the bills and coins currently in **circulation**. However, our money didn't always look like it does today.

Before the United States was officially a country, the Continental Congress issued paper money called *continentals*. Because no one was sure that America could gain its independence, continentals weren't worth very much. Shortly after America won its independence, the first dollar coins were struck.

A four dollar continental currency printed in 1776.

Since then, American currency has been a mix of bills and coins of various **denominations**.

In 1789, the Treasury Department was created. It regulates the printing of paper money and the minting of coins.

Alexander Hamilton was the first United States Secretary of the Treasury, serving from 1789 to 1795.

5

Making Coins:
The United States Mint

The main job of the United States **Mint** is to produce enough coins to keep American businesses running smoothly. That is a huge job! In the year 2000, the mint had to produce 28 billion coins!

Most coins are minted in three U.S. Mint facilities. They are located in Philadelphia, Pennsylvania; Denver, Colorado; and San Francisco, California. A mint in West Point, New York, produces special coins made of gold, silver, and platinum.

6

Philadelphia, Pennsylvania

Denver, Colorado

San Francisco, California

Designing Coins

The words In God We Trust *appear on all U.S. currency.*

It is up to Congress to decide when to create a new coin design or to issue a new coin or medal. When that happens, the **engravers** at the United States Mint spring into action. First, a design is approved and sculpted into a clay model. These models are usually much larger than the coin they will eventually become.

Next, several plaster models are made by pouring plaster over the clay model. Then epoxy is used to make a very strong and durable model.

Finally, a metal **die** is engraved from the epoxy model. One die is made for the front of the coin, and another is made for the back. Together, these dies will be used to stamp the image on the coin.

9

Obverse and Reverse

When you flip a coin, you call heads or tails. If it lands on heads, the **obverse**, or front, of the coin faces up. The obverse of a coin shows a portrait of a famous historical figure. If the coin lands on tails, the **reverse**, or back, of the coin is showing. The picture on the reverse is usually related to the picture on the obverse. For example, the obverse of a penny shows a portrait of Abraham Lincoln, and the reverse shows a picture of the Lincoln Memorial.

The quarter is different. From 1999 to 2008, a new design for each of the fifty states appeared on the reverse. Every ten weeks, a new state was honored.

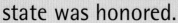

The designs of current United States coins show many important historical people and places.

Did you know...

Did you know that there are six elements that must appear on every coin design? They include the year the coin was issued and its denomination, as well as the following phrases:

Liberty

In God We Trust

United States of America

E Pluribus Unum (Latin for 'From Many, One')

11

The Six-Step Process

Before a coin ever makes it into your pocket, it goes through a six-step process to make sure it meets the high standards of the U.S. Mint.

A coin begins its life as part of a long coil of metal. These coils, or strips, of metal, are over a foot (.3 m) wide and more than 1,500 feet (457 m) long. Once these strips arrive at the mint, the process begins.

STEP ONE: BLANKING

The long coils of metal are fed into a blanking press, where they can be punched into blanks the size of the coin they will become.

STEP TWO: ANNEALING, WASHING, AND DRYING

Annealing is a process that uses heat to make the blanks soft enough to work with. The blanks are then washed and dried to remove debris from their surface.

STEP THREE: UPSETTING

A slight rim is created on the edge of each blank by running it through an upsetting mill.

STEP FOUR: STRIKING

The blanks are finally ready to become coins. They are run through a **press**, where they are struck on both sides with the dies that create their unique designs.

14

STEP FIVE: INSPECTION

After emerging from the press, the newly minted coins are inspected with a magnifying glass to make sure they were struck properly. Coins that do not meet standards are removed.

STEP SIX: COUNTING

Coins are counted automatically by machine. Then they are placed in bags and transported to banks. From there, they are placed in circulation, and some end up in your pockets!

Coin Errors

Millions of coins are minted each day. Not all of these are perfect. Coins that do not meet standards of the United States Mint are called errors. Most errors are caught at the inspection stage, but some make it into circulation.

Because errors are rare, some coins with errors can be worth a great deal of money. For example, a few 1969-S Lincoln pennies were struck twice. If you can find one of these rare coins, you can sell it for tens of thousands of dollars!

It's easy to spot the doubling of the letters and numbers on this 1955 penny.

Famous Coin Errors

1937-D 3-Leg Indian Head Nickel—In this coin, the front leg of the buffalo appears to be missing.

1943 Copper Cent—During World War II, copper was hard to find, so pennies were minted in steel. A few copper pennies were minted by mistake. Only about twelve are known to exist. One recently sold for over $200,000!

2007 Godless Dollar—The dollars are called godless because the words *In God We Trust* are missing from the rim where they were supposed to appear.

Making Paper Money: The Bureau of Engraving and Printing

Both the United States Mint and the Bureau of Engraving and Printing (BEP) produce U.S. currency. The difference is that the Mint produces coins, and the BEP is responsible for producing all of America's paper money. Like the Mint, the BEP is part of the Department of the Treasury.

The BEP prints **notes**, or bills, in denominations of $1, $2, $5, $10, $20, $50, and $100. The largest bill ever produced was the $100,000 Gold Certificate printed in 1934.

All the paper money in the United States is produced in two facilities. One is in Washington, D.C., and the other is in Fort Worth, Texas.

19

Designing Bills

Like coins, paper money must be designed. A number of engravers will work on the design of a typical bill. One may work on the portrait, another on the picture on the back of the bill, and  still others may work on the different kinds of lettering you see on each note.

The engravers create a master die by hand cutting their designs into a soft steel plate. The master die is then used to create a plate with thirty-two impressions of the original. This is used to print bills.

By law, bills must be designed with certain features. The words *In God We Trust* must appear on every bill. The portraits on notes may not be of living people.

The Faces on Bills

$1

George Washington

First President

$2

Thomas Jefferson

Third President

$5

Abraham Lincoln

Sixteenth President

$10

Alexander Hamilton

First Secretary of the Treasury

$20

Andrew Jackson

Seventh President

$50

Ulysses S. Grant

Eighteenth President

$100

Benjamin Franklin

Founding Father

Paper and Ink

The most interesting fact about the paper used to make United States bills is that it isn't paper at all! What we call paper money is actually made of cloth. It is a mix of 75 percent cotton and 25 percent linen. This combination makes our bills strong, to resist wear and tear. It also gives our money a unique feel that helps people tell real money from fake money.

All bills are the same size. They measure 6.14 inches by 2.61 inches (15.6 cm by 6.6 cm). Each bill weighs one gram, so one pound of bills should contain 454 bills (454 grams = 1 pound).

American bills have long been called *greenbacks*. This is because all our paper bills use green ink on the reverse side. Black ink is used on the front.

Features that use different colors, such as serial numbers and the colored seal on bills, are printed separately.

The Printing Process

Our bills are beautifully detailed. The designs have many dots and fine lines both on the front and back. In order to make these details stand out, a printing process known as **intaglio** is used.

The printing press is loaded with thousands of sheets of paper. Each sheet will contain 32 bills. The paper is fed into the press under tremendous pressure to make sure the fine details appear.

A press can produce bills at an incredible rate of speed. Up to 10,000 sheets can be printed per hour. First, the backs are printed with green ink. Then the sheets are stacked and allowed to dry before the fronts are printed with black ink. After another drying period, the Treasury seal and the serial numbers are printed on the bills.

The sheets are inspected to make sure that there are no errors. Defective sheets are discarded. The remaining sheets are sent along to the last step in the bill-making process.

Cutting the Bills

Once the sheets have been dried and inspected, they must be cut into bills. Stacks of one hundred sheets are gathered together and cut to exact size. Once the bills are cut, they are formed into stacks of one hundred notes each. Forty stacks are packaged together into a brick containing 4,000 notes. At this point, the bills are ready to go into circulation.

Putting Paper Money into Circulation

In order to get from the printing press to your pocket, paper money must be put into circulation. To do this, bricks of notes are transported to each of the twelve Federal Reserve banks around the country.

The Federal Reserve banks then distribute the money to local banks, which put the money into circulation.

27

Preventing Counterfeiting

As long as paper money has existed, criminals have tried to make **counterfeit**, or fake, bills. Modern computers, scanners, and printers have made counterfeiting much easier to attempt. However, the BEP has added many **security** features to bills to make sure you can recognize real money when you see it.

Prior to 1996, the BEP added two important security features:

Security Thread: All bills with denominations of $5 or greater contain a thin thread that glows different colors when held under an ultraviolet light.

Microprinting: This is lettering so small that it appears to be a line, but when you magnify it the letters appear. It is difficult for computer printers to copy such small lettering.

28

The BEP is always trying to stay ahead of counterfeiters. Since 1996, many new security features have been introduced.

Large Portraits: These have been enlarged to allow for more detail.

Color Shifting Ink: The color of the numeral in the lower right corner of bills changes color as you look at it from different angles.

Watermark: This is a very faint image that can be seen in strong light but can't be easily copied.

Low Vision Feature: This large numeral on the back of bills helps those who have difficulty seeing, but the colored ink helps stop counterfeiters, as well.

Money Facts

The way money looks has changed a great deal since it was first printed in the United States. Still, money is made in much the same way it used to be. Even with all of today's technology, we rely on printing presses and mints just as we did when the first U.S. money was produced.

- The first coin presses at the United States Mint were operated by horses and oxen.

- The average coin lasts about thirty years, but the average bill lasts only about a year and a half.

- The mint mark on coins tells you which mint it came from. S stands for San Francisco, D stands for Denver, and P stands for Philadelphia. Coins from the Philadelphia mint often have no mint mark at all.

- The Bureau of Engraving and Printing started out with just six employees in 1871.

- More than 80 billion dollars worth of notes can be printed in a single year. Most of these notes are made to replace older, worn out notes.

30

Glossary

circulation (sur-kyuh-LAY-shun): the amount of bills and coins in use

counterfeit (KOUN-tur-fit): something that has been made to look like the real thing but is fake, such as counterfeit money

denominations (di-nom-uh-NAY-shuhns): values or units in a system of measurement

die (DYE): an engraved stamp for impressing a design on soft materials

engravers (en-GRAYV-urz): people who cut a design or letters into a surface

intaglio (in-TAHL-yoh): an engraving process that allows ink to stay in the grooves and be transferred onto paper

mint (MINT): a place where coins are manufactured

notes (NOHTS): pieces of paper money

obverse (OB-vurss): the front of a coin or bill

press (PRESS): a machine that uses force to press an image on a coin

reverse (ri-VURSS): the back of a coin or bill

security (si-KYOOR-uh-tee): making secure or safe

Index

Further Reading

Cribb, Joe. *Money*. DK Children, 2005.

Lange, David W. *History of The United States Mint and Its Coinage*.
Whitman Publishing, 2005.

Websites

www.moneyfactory.gov/

www.usmint.gov/

www.pbs.org/wgbh/nova/moolah/anatomy.html

About the Author

Tim Clifford is an educational writer and the author of many non-fiction children's books. He has two wonderful daughters and two energetic Border Collies that he adopted from a shelter. Tim became a vegetarian because of his love for animals. He is also a computer nut and a sports fanatic. He lives and works in New York City as a public school teacher.

32